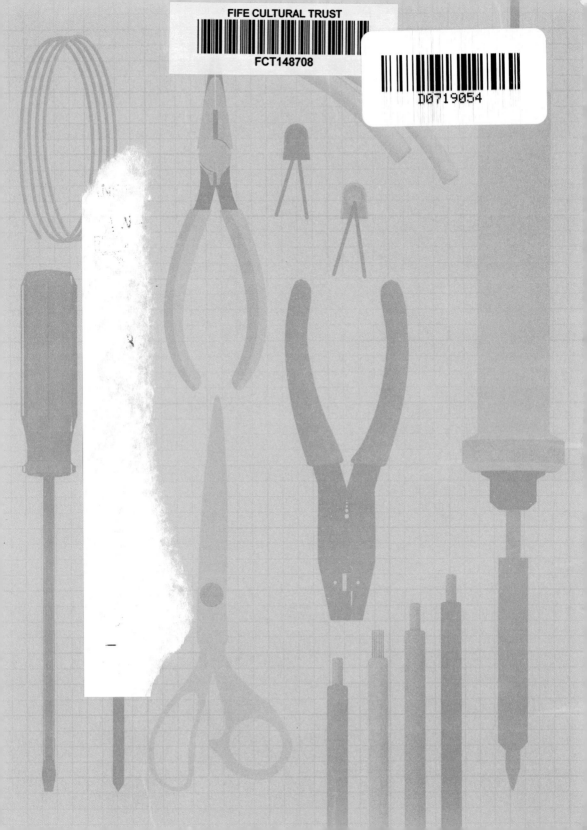

The GADGET INVENTOR Handbook

MIKE WARREN

Quarto is the authority on a wide range of topics.

Quarto educates, entertains and enriches the lives of our readers—enthusiasts and lovers of hands-on living.

www.quartoknows.com

Author: Mike Warren
Illustrator: Antony Evans/Beehive Illustration
Editorial Director: Laura Knowles
Art Director: Susi Martin
Publisher: Maxime Boucknooghe
Designed and edited by Tall Tree Ltd

ISBN: 978-1-78493-781-2

Printed and bound in China by Toppan Leefung

10 9 8 7 6 5 4 3 2 1   16 17 18 19 20

Contents

Are you ready to build gadgets?

Electronics projects are fun to make and easy to build. You can find most of the small bits and pieces needed to make them inside other electronic gadgets. These components can be put together in an almost endless number of ways to create a huge range of electronic gizmos.

For this book, the circuits and components have been kept simple. You'll also see that many of the components are used in several gadgets so that you can learn how to use and connect them quickly and easily. The next few pages will show you some essential gadget-building techniques.

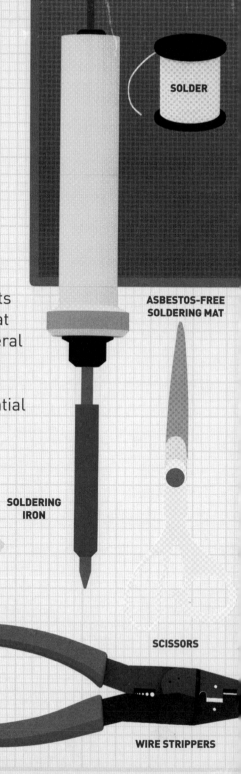

SOLDER

ASBESTOS-FREE
SOLDERING MAT

SOLDERING
IRON

HEAT-SHRINK TUBING

WIRE CUTTERS

SCISSORS

ELECTRICAL WIRE

WIRE STRIPPERS

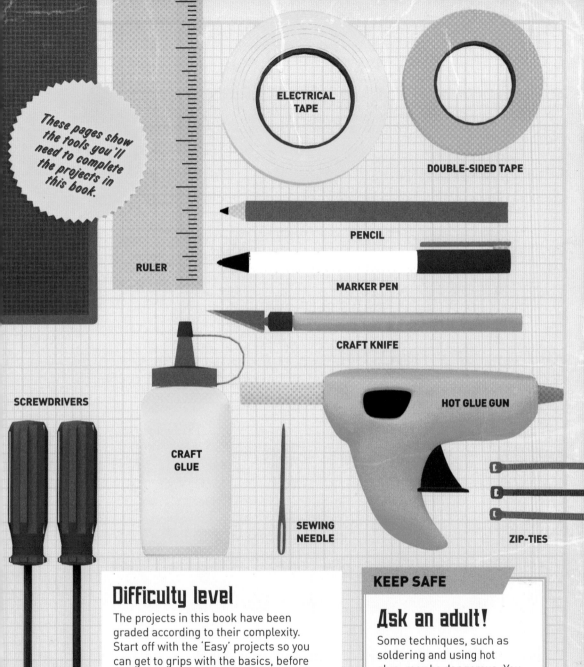

These pages show the tools you'll need to complete the projects in this book.

ELECTRICAL TAPE

DOUBLE-SIDED TAPE

PENCIL

MARKER PEN

RULER

CRAFT KNIFE

SCREWDRIVERS

CRAFT GLUE

HOT GLUE GUN

SEWING NEEDLE

ZIP-TIES

Difficulty level

The projects in this book have been graded according to their complexity. Start off with the 'Easy' projects so you can get to grips with the basics, before moving on to 'Intermediate' and finally tackling the 'Advanced' activities.

EASY

INTERMEDIATE

ADVANCED

KEEP SAFE

Ask an adult!

Some techniques, such as soldering and using hot glue, may be dangerous. You should get the help of an adult wherever you see this symbol.

What is a circuit?

An electrical circuit is much like a race track, where runners start and finish a race at the same point. In an electrical circuit, the battery is the start of the race, the power goes through various components and ends up back at the battery again. If the power leaves the battery and doesn't make it back, then the circuit is incomplete, or broken. This is called an open circuit.

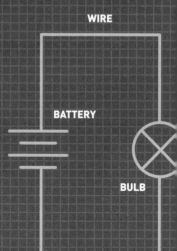

WIRE

BATTERY

BULB

Turn it on!

We all know that light switches turn lights on and off, but what they are really doing is breaking the circuit or flow of electricity. There are lots of types of switch, but in this book we'll be dealing with Single Pole Single Throw (SPST) switches, Single Pole Double Throw (SPDT) switches and Momentary switches.

SPST SWITCH

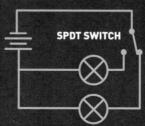

SPDT SWITCH

SPST

SPST are among the most common types of switch, and can be found in lights and fans. Single pole means there's only one way to pull the switch (on/off), and the single throw means it only affects one circuit. An SPDT switch controls two circuits.

Momentary switches

Momentary switches complete a circuit, but only for a moment. These switches work only when they are pressed, which makes them perfect for electronic projects where we want power at a specific time.

Pins

If you examine a switch, you'll notice on the underside that there are small indents and notes written to give you clues to how the switch operates. Typically, switches will have a side that power goes into and a side where power leaves from. No matter how many pins there are, there will be clues on the switch that indicate where you need to wire.

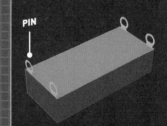

PIN

Amps, volts and resistance

WIRE

+

BATTERY

-

BULB

When we talk about electricity, we need to think about voltage, current and resistance. Imagine a large tank of water with a small hose coming out the bottom of the tank.

We know that pressure at the end of the hose will be different from the pressure at the top of the tank. If water was pouring out of the hose, the pressure measured at the end of the hose would be the voltage.

Electrical resistance is like an obstacle in the hose, it will restrict the flow of water.

The width of the hose will determine how much water can escape – this is the current (amps).

Current can be Alternating Current (AC) or Direct Current (DC). Alternating Current flows out and reverses direction many times a second – it alternates. This is the type of power that's in the wall outlets in your home. Direct Current only flows in one direction – it is direct. For the projects in this book, you'll be using batteries, which provide DC power.

Never try to conduct any of the projects here with any other power supply than what is specified, and never attempt to plug anything into a wall socket.

WHICH WAY ROUND?

Polarity of batteries

Now that we know that DC current flows in one direction, we can discuss polarity. If you look at a battery, you can see it has two terminals. These terminals have symbols next to them indicating the positive (+) side and the negative (-) side. These are the poles of the battery.

For some components, it doesn't matter which direction the power flows. For other components, such as LEDs, electrical charge needs to travel in a specific direction. If you are having trouble getting your circuit to work correctly, you may have your component connected the wrong way. Try turning it around so the polarity is correct.

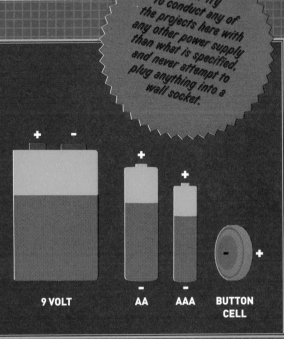

+ -

+

+

- +

9 VOLT   AA   AAA   BUTTON CELL

Types of circuit

When wiring more than one component into a circuit, there are two basic ways to complete the wiring – in parallel or in series.

Breadboards

Breadboards are a great way to test your wiring before you start soldering. They work by supplying positive (+) and negative (-) power outlets to the outer rails running down either side, as shown with red (+) and blue (-) lines (see image, right). Power can then be drawn from these sides into the middle section, where the power runs across the breadboard.

Series

Wiring in series is like a daisy-chain, where each successive component is attached to the previous one. This means each component in the series receives the same amount of current (amps). The drawback to this type of wiring is that if one component fails along the chain, then the entire chain breaks, and the circuit is left open.

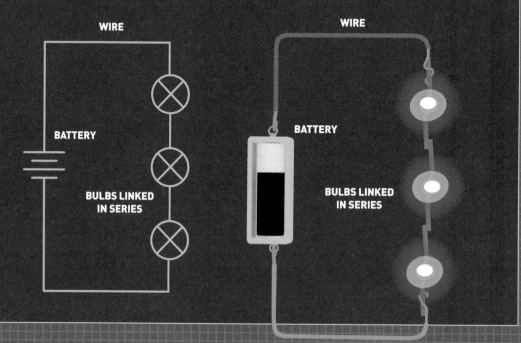

WIRE

BATTERY

BULBS LINKED
IN SERIES

WIRE

BATTERY

BULBS LINKED
IN SERIES

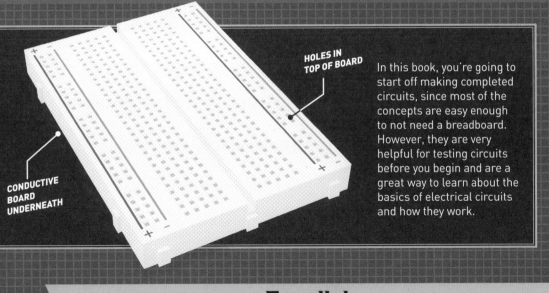

HOLES IN
TOP OF BOARD

CONDUCTIVE
BOARD
UNDERNEATH

In this book, you're going to start off making completed circuits, since most of the concepts are easy enough to not need a breadboard. However, they are very helpful for testing circuits before you begin and are a great way to learn about the basics of electrical circuits and how they work.

Parallel

Wiring things in parallel is like stacking components, where each component is arranged to share polarity on a common side, and they all receive the same voltage. If one component fails in a parallel circuit, the rest of the circuit still works.

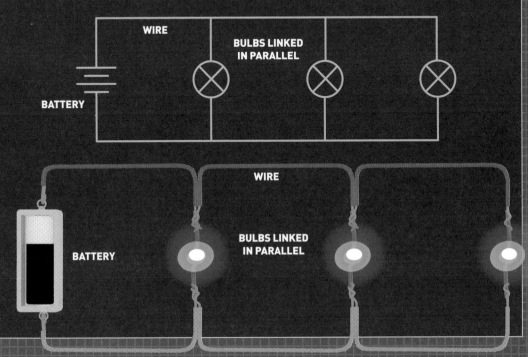

WIRE

BULBS LINKED
IN PARALLEL

BATTERY

WIRE

BULBS LINKED
IN PARALLEL

BATTERY

Stripping wires

Wires are the connections between various components. Preparing them so that they can be joined is a key part of making an electrical circuit.

Wires are protected by an insulating plastic or vinyl jacket. This makes sure that they don't come into contact with something they shouldn't do and create a short circuit. However, in order to make a circuit, you need to strip away part of the jacket to expose the wiring. It's a simple job, but takes a little bit of practice to ensure that you're able to strip the right amount of wire for the right job.

You will need

- **electrical wires**
- **wire cutters**
- **wire strippers**

How to cut wires

When cutting wires, always cut a longer length than you think you need. You can always trim more off later, but you can't add more. Take time to measure out your wires, and always have a few wires of different colours to help keep your project organized. The wires inside may look a little different, but they will all conduct electricity in the same way and can be used for the projects in this book.

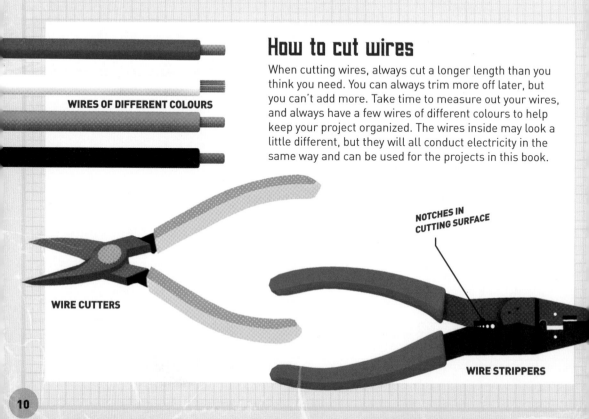

WIRES OF DIFFERENT COLOURS

NOTCHES IN CUTTING SURFACE

WIRE CUTTERS

WIRE STRIPPERS

How to strip wire ends

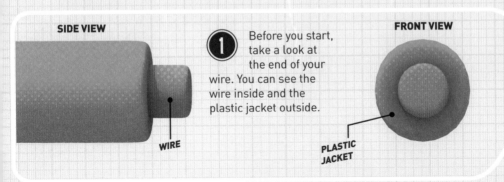

SIDE VIEW

FRONT VIEW

1 Before you start, take a look at the end of your wire. You can see the wire inside and the plastic jacket outside.

WIRE

PLASTIC JACKET

2 A wire stripper is the best tool to remove the plastic jacket. It looks a little bit like a pair of short scissors and has different size notches on the cutting edge. These fit around the wire and cut into the plastic jacket without damaging the wire inside. Since wires are different diameters, it's important to find the right size notch in the strippers.

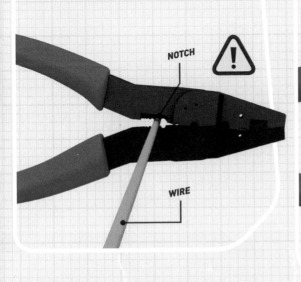

NOTCH

WIRE

3 When removing the jacket from the wire ends, try to keep the section you strip to about 1 cm long. By keeping the amount of wire exposed to a minimum, you reduce the chance of stray components making contact with the wire and shorting out your circuit.

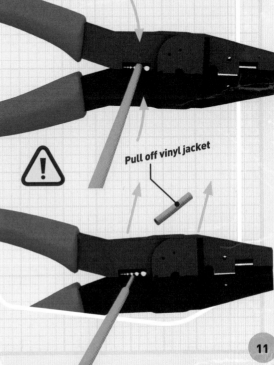

Pull off vinyl jacket

How to solder

Soldering uses heat and a metal with a low melting point to join things, such as wires, together. The heat comes from a soldering iron and the metal is usually a material called solder. As the solder cools, it hardens and bonds the two things together. Soldering is very strong and will prevent wires from coming apart, and since solder is conductive, it can be used to create a complete circuit.

You will need

- **soldering iron**
- **solder**
- **soldering mat**
- **soldering extractor fan**
- **soldering tip cleaner**

Let's go!

Helping hands

Sometimes, there are too many things to hold at once and you may need these tools, known as 'helping hands'. They can hold your bits and pieces in place while you handle the iron and solder.

 1 Before you start soldering, make sure that your workstation is set up correctly.

- Keep the area clear of any clutter.
- Use a solid mat to work on. Make sure that it is made from a material that doesn't conduct electricity or heat, such as ceramic or carbon fibre and not metal or wood.
- Make sure there is plenty of ventilation to get rid of the small amount of smoke. Some set-ups include a vent hood that extracts the smoke, but an open window and an extractor fan work well too.
- Use a soldering tip cleaner to keep your iron clean for each new job.

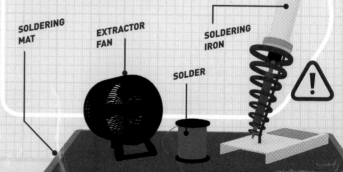

SOLDERING MAT

EXTRACTOR FAN

SOLDER

SOLDERING IRON

2 After you have a soldering space cleared, plug in your soldering iron and wait for it to heat up. Attempting to solder before the iron is hot enough will not work. Give the iron at least 1 minute to warm up to the right temperature. While the iron is warming up you can start setting up what you want to solder.

3 Twist the exposed ends of two wires together. Then apply the tip of the soldering iron to the twisted wires and allow a few seconds for the items being soldered to heat up.

Heat up the exposed wires with the soldering iron

4 Feed in a small amount of solder to the tip of the iron. The solder will melt and trickle on to the items being soldered. It's really that easy!

Add the solder

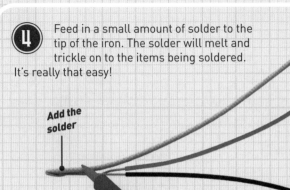

Troubleshooter

Did you make a mistake? No problem – correcting things can be just as easy! You could just trim away the mistake and start again. Or you can de-solder the join. Start by applying heat to melt the solder and gently pull on the items to release them. De-soldering can be tricky with more complex soldering jobs, so it's always good to practise soldering before starting a project.

TAKE IT FURTHER

How to tin wires

You may find it easier to tin your wire ends before soldering. In tinning, solder is applied to only one of the wires and allowed to cool – that wire is now ready to be joined to another wire. When you're ready to solder, you just have to hold the two wires next to each other and re-melt the cooled solder on the first wire. As the solder cools again, it joins the two wires together.

LED throwie

LED throwies are a low-cost, no-solder electronic gizmo that can be made in seconds. They stick to any ferromagnetic surface, such as your fridge or a car, and are a great way to add a bit of fun and colour around your home.

You will need

- **LED (the bigger the better, look for a 10 mm one)**
- **button cell battery (like the ones for watches)**
- **small rare-earth magnet**
- **tape**

How to make your throwies

Troubleshooter

If your LED doesn't light up immediately then maybe you've got the leads the wrong way round. Try flipping the LED round and touching the leads to the other terminals on the battery. When the LED is lit up you can check the colour and brightness.

These LED throwies can last up to a week, so choose where you throw them carefully!

① Place the LED over the button cell battery with the cathode and anode leads touching the terminals on either side. The longer LED lead is the anode and should be touching the positive (+) side of the battery.

② With the LED in place, use a small piece of tape to fix the leads to the battery. Remember to wrap the tape tightly to create a secure connection between the LED and the battery.

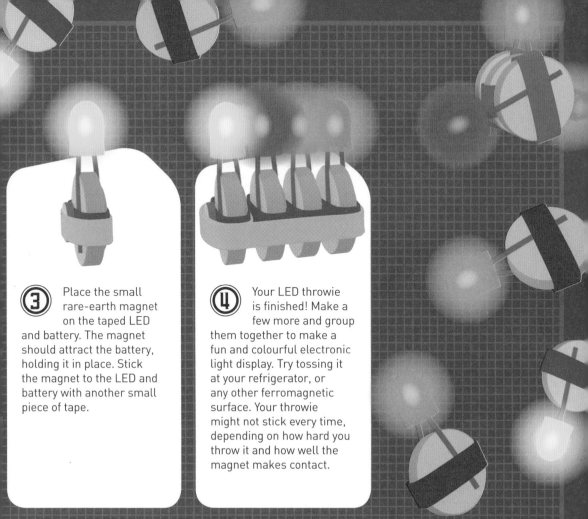

3 Place the small rare-earth magnet on the taped LED and battery. The magnet should attract the battery, holding it in place. Stick the magnet to the LED and battery with another small piece of tape.

4 Your LED throwie is finished! Make a few more and group them together to make a fun and colourful electronic light display. Try tossing it at your refrigerator, or any other ferromagnetic surface. Your throwie might not stick every time, depending on how hard you throw it and how well the magnet makes contact.

TAKE IT FURTHER

Blinky throwies

You can also buy LEDs that 'blink' when they are switched on. Why not add one to this project and make your LED blink away. Because of the flashing light, they use less energy from the battery, allowing this LED throwie to last even longer!

LED floatie

The LED floatie is like your LED throwie, except it is without a magnet and is put inside a balloon. Assemble an LED throwie and put it inside an uninflated balloon. Blow up the balloon and tie the neck off, securing your lit-up LED inside. The LED floatie can then be placed in a pond to create a colourful glow!

Try mixing up the LED colours with different balloon colours to create an even more interesting effect. Just remember to collect your balloons afterwards and never leave any rubbish after you've had your fun. Wildlife and balloons don't mix!

Mini vibrating robot

This cute little robot is easy to make and only requires four things to build. Why not build a few and battle your friends to push each other out of the ring in a mini game of sumo wrestling.

You will need

- **small vibrating motor (vibrating motors can be found in electric toothbrushes)**
- **toothbrush**
- **button cell battery**
- **double-sided tape**

Building time!

1 Cut off the head of the toothbrush. If you have an old vibrating toothbrush you can open it up and find the vibrating motor inside. Break the body open and remove the motor with the wires attached.

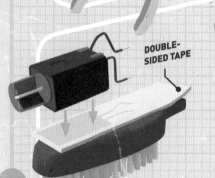

MOTOR

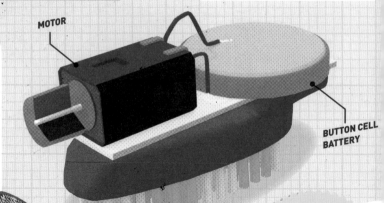

BUTTON CELL BATTERY

This robot lets you collect many of your key components from the same device!

DOUBLE-SIDED TAPE

2 Place a small piece of double-sided tape on the flat back of the toothbrush head. Push the vibrating motor down onto the tape with the rotating end facing the tip of the toothbrush head.

3 Strip the end of one of the vibrating motor wires and place it on the tape at the cut end of the toothbrush. Then place the battery directly on top of the exposed wire.

4 When you're ready to activate the robot, place the other motor wire on top of the battery to complete the circuit and bring your robot to life! This little critter will vibrate as long as there is a connection between the motor and the battery, or until the battery runs out of power. To stop the robot, just move the top wire so it no longer connects with the battery.

Sumo match!

If you make a few of these simple robots you can have a sumo wrestling match with your friends. Take a dinner plate and place it on the floor upside down. Put the vibrating robots on the plate at the same time and see which one can stay on the plate for the longest.

TAKE IT FURTHER

BIG vibrating robot

This is the big brother of the mini vibrating robot. We'll use the same principles, but with larger components and a few twists that will make this robot even more fun to play with.

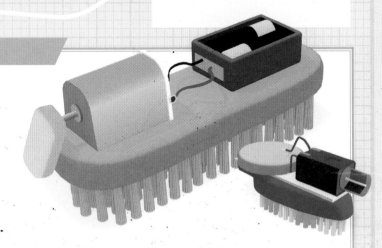

You will need

- **large scrubbing brush with bristles**
- **hobby motor (like those in small personal fans - ideally using 2 AA batteries)**
- **one 2 AA battery holder**
- **pencil eraser**

1 You can find hobby motors that run on batteries in loads of electronics, like personal fans or toy cars. A good place to source supplies cheaply is a charity shop or discount bin at a department store. You'll need the motor and the wire leads coming from it, so keep them intact when you remove them.

2 Carefully strip the ends of the motor wires and the battery holder wires, then solder the black wires together and the red wires together. This is a complete circuit and the batteries will power the motor when they are inserted.

3 Hot glue the motor to the flat back of the large scrubbing brush at one end, with the motor shaft over the edge. Then glue the battery holder to the other end of the flat top of the scrubbing brush.

4 To make the mini robot move, you used an off-balance weight on the motor. To do this on the larger motor, you need to add a weight. An eraser makes an ideal weight. Push it onto the motor shaft and make sure that it is slightly off-centre to create an off-balance effect. Put the batteries into the battery holder and watch it go!

DIY switch

Switches can be found in almost every electronic device, and you can easily take switches from broken or cheap electronics. To really understand the science behind why switches work, however, it's better to make your own switch.

This switch is operated by making contact between two parts of a circuit, but only when held in place by the user. This type of switch is called a momentary switch.

This switch can be added to any of the projects in this book.

Turn it on!

You will need

- **craft foam sheet**
- **aluminium foil**
- **2 paperclips**
- **electrical wire**
- **glue**
- **scissors**
- **pencil**
- **ruler**

1 Cut three identical 8 cm x 8 cm squares from the craft foam, then cut two squares of aluminium foil measuring 7 cm x 7 cm.

8 CM

7 CM

2 Place a paperclip over one edge of a foam square, then repeat for a second foam square. Glue a foil square in the centre of each of the foam squares, so that the lower half of each paperclip is covered.

Turn to page 6 to find out about other types of switch.

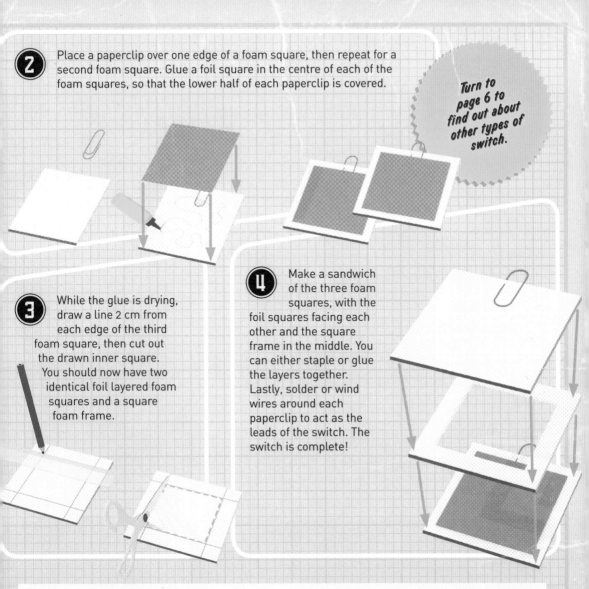

3 While the glue is drying, draw a line 2 cm from each edge of the third foam square, then cut out the drawn inner square. You should now have two identical foil layered foam squares and a square foam frame.

4 Make a sandwich of the three foam squares, with the foil squares facing each other and the square frame in the middle. You can either staple or glue the layers together. Lastly, solder or wind wires around each paperclip to act as the leads of the switch. The switch is complete!

How it works

When you push down on the centre of the top foam square, the foil sheets come into contact with each other, completing the circuit. When you let go of the switch, the foam sheet springs back, pulling the foil sheets apart, and the circuit becomes open. Attach your wires to a battery and a small light to make a simple circuit.

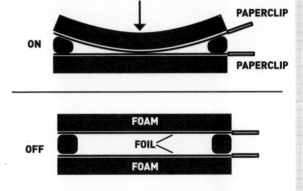

ON

PAPERCLIP

PAPERCLIP

OFF

FOAM

FOIL

FOAM

Personal doorbell

RING BELL TO ENTER!

A doorbell is great for when someone is at your front door, but how about when they're at the door to your very own room? Take your electronics game up a notch by making an easy doorbell to hang outside your room. This will let you know when someone wants to come in.

You will need

- **9 volt electric buzzer**
- **9 volt battery**
- **9 volt snap connector**
- **doorbell switch**
- **electrical wire**
- **soldering iron and solder**

A doorbell is really just another type of switch. It completes a circuit when you press it and chimes a bell to let you know it's been rung.

① Start by soldering long wires onto each terminal of the doorbell switch. Cut the wires so that they are long enough for you to place your doorbell wherever you want.

SWITCH

② Solder one of the long doorbell switch wires to the positive (+) wire of the 9 volt snap connector. Then solder the other doorbell switch wire to the positive buzzer wire.

③ Next, solder the negative (-) buzzer wire to the negative wire of the 9 volt snap connector. Buzzers have polarity, so having the battery connection match the buzzer polarity is very important.

BUZZER

9 VOLT SNAP CONNECTOR

④ Connecting the 9 volt battery to the snap connector will power the circuit. You can test your doorbell now to see if the buzzer sounds when the doorbell is pressed.

There are many types of buzzer available, and they will all have different voltages. This project needs a low voltage buzzer, so look for something under 9 volts. You will need a battery that works with whichever type of buzzer you have.

⑤ With the longer wires soldered in place, you can place the doorbell outside your room on the door frame and have the buzzer and battery secured inside your room on the other side of the frame.

BATTERY

LED bracelet

Bring your fashion bling out of the darkness with a colourful LED bracelet. You can customize this e-textile accessory with any number of LEDs so that you really stand out from the crowd.

Vary the number and colour of the LEDs on your bracelet to see what works best with your favourite outfits.

You will need

- **felt strip (about 10 cm wide)**
- **button cell battery holder**
- **button cell battery**
- **3 LEDs**
- **needle**
- **conductive thread**
- **cotton thread**
- **button snaps**

It's glow time!

1 Wrap the felt strip around your wrist to see how much you'll need so that your bracelet sits comfortably. Then cut it to the right length, leaving enough material so that the two ends overlap a little.

10 CM

Work on this side

2 Mentally divide the felt strip in half along its length. You'll be working on one side of this line, installing all your components, and then folding the other side over to cover the electronics. So the final bracelet will be 5 cm wide when you're finished.

3 Poke one LED through the felt in the middle of the half you are working on, then poke the other LEDs on either side about 3 cm apart. Make sure that the positive (+) legs of the LEDs are facing towards the long edge of the felt. Using long nose pliers, twist the LED legs into a tight curl. This will secure the LEDs to the felt.

– +

Decorate the band of your bracelet using felt markers, glitter and stickers. Change the position of the LEDs so that they work with your design.

4 Sew the button cell battery holder to one end of the felt on the same side as the curled legs of the LEDs.

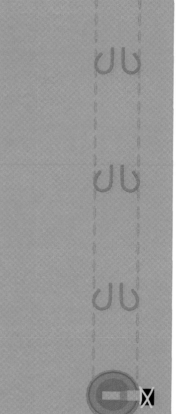

5 Using conductive thread, sew from the positive terminal of the battery holder straight down the length of the felt joining the positive (+) legs of the LEDs. Then sew another line of thread connecting the negative terminal of the battery holder to the negative (-) legs of the LEDs. The LEDs are now wired together in parallel.

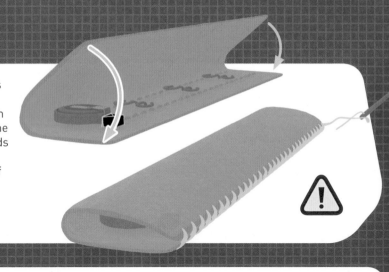

6. Fold the felt lengthways to cover the battery holder. Then run a stitch along the long edge to secure the folded felt, leaving the short ends open. The button snaps will be added close to the short ends of the folded felt.

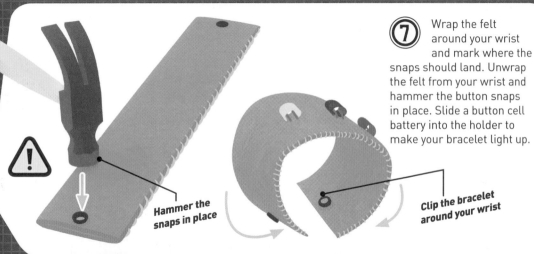

7. Wrap the felt around your wrist and mark where the snaps should land. Unwrap the felt from your wrist and hammer the button snaps in place. Slide a button cell battery into the holder to make your bracelet light up.

Hammer the snaps in place

Clip the bracelet around your wrist

TAKE IT FURTHER

Taking control

Since the ends of the felt bracelet are left open, the battery can be inserted into the holder to activate the LEDs. If you wanted to take this project to the next level you can introduce a SPST switch (see page 6). For an even more technical challenge, how about trying to use the snaps as the switch?

You can transfer the concepts of this bracelet into other clothes to make anything you're wearing light up!

Rough 'n' ready race car

Making your own motorised model race car is super easy and, just like the real thing, there's no end to the tweaking and modifying you can do to improve its performance.

This car will use two small hobby motors to power the rear wheels, with two freely rotating wheels at the front. These are all housed in a sturdy chassis to hold the batteries. Customize your chassis for better speed and style, then race against your friends!

You will need

- **2 motors**
- **juice carton**
- **4 wheels (bottle tops or hobby wheels)**
- **batteries (to suit the motors used)**
- **battery holder**
- **electrical wire**
- **SPDT switch**
- **breadboard**
- **solder**
- **hot glue**
- **elastic bands**
- **pencil**

Finding your motors

The speed of your racer will mainly be determined by the motors. Find two identical motors and match them to the appropriate type and number of batteries. You can find motors in small cheap electronic items, such as fans or small toys. Best of all, the motors salvaged from these cheap items will have the suitable batteries already worked out.

Try using wheels of different sizes and see if they affect how fast your race car goes.

Construction instructions!

1 Match the batteries to your motors and place them in a battery holder to keep them together. This will make it much easier to wire them to the motors.

Add a racing wing to give your car extra grip

Turn to pages 8–9 to get to grips with using a breadboard.

2 Test the wiring on a breadboard, which is an electronic circuit builder. Start by attaching the batteries to the positive and negative rails of the breadboard, then follow the wiring diagram below to test out the circuit.

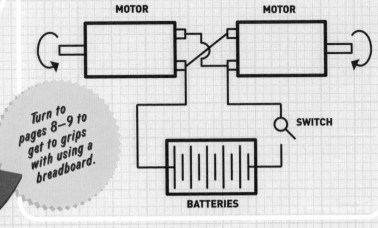

MOTOR   MOTOR

SWITCH

BATTERIES

3 Turn on the switch and see the direction your motors are turning and how fast. To make the rotation easier to spot, you can add a small piece of adhesive tape to each motor shaft. Since these motors will be on opposite sides of the racer, you'll need the motors to spin in opposite directions. You can easily change the motor rotation by swapping the power wires to the motor, which reverses the polarity.

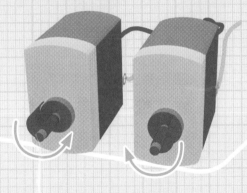

4 When you are satisfied with your breadboard test, you can solder the connections together permanently. Make sure to remove the batteries from the battery holder before you start soldering to prevent any short circuits.

5 Now you can make the chassis (the frame the car is built around). Cut one large side of the juice box off. Then clean and dry the insides. Poke two small openings either side of the back end of the box for the motor shafts to stick out of. Poke two openings in either side of the front end for the front wheels.

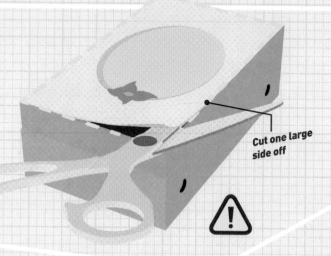

Cut one large side off

6 Using hot glue, carefully attach the motors inside the juice box, paying close attention to the rotational direction of the motors and making sure you avoid getting any glue near the motor shaft. Glue in the battery holder and find a suitable location to place the switch. You may need to poke another hole in the side if you want your switch on the outside of your car.

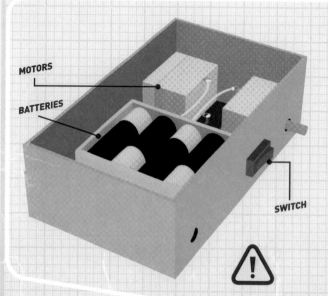

MOTORS

BATTERIES

SWITCH

Ask an adult to help you when you are using hot glue or solder. Don't forget to follow the soldering instructions on pages 12–13.

7 Now all that's left is to decide on wheels. Many hobby shops sell an assortment of wheels, but you can also make your own wheels from bottle tops. Increase the traction by wrapping each bottle top with elastic bands.

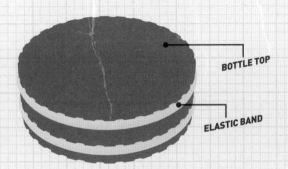

BOTTLE TOP

ELASTIC BAND

8 Stick a pencil through the holes at the front of the juice box. Make sure that the holes are large enough so that the pencil will be able to turn easily as the racing car moves along. Use hot glue to stick the ends of the pencil to the two front wheels. Glue the rear wheels to the ends of the motor shafts.

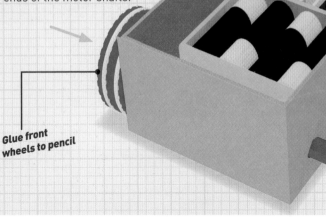

Glue front wheels to pencil

9 Decorate your car to finish it, then place it on the ground and push the switch to make it go! Challenge your friends to see whose racer is the fastest, or can go the furthest when sent up a ramp.

TAKE IT FURTHER

Switch the chassis

Once you've mastered the motorised part of your race car, you can experiment with making your chassis in different shapes and out of different materials. Do some materials allow your car to zoom along more quickly? Are some shapes more stable than others? Don't forget to decorate your car with some bright racing colours and go-faster stripes!

Drawing with light

You've had fun with the basics of LEDs by making LED throwies (see pages 14–15). Now it's time to take it up a level by making light pens that will allow you to draw in the dark! You'll be using the same concept as the LED throwie, but introducing wires and a switch into the circuit. This will give you control over the LED operation and allow you to put everything into a tidy package.

You will need

- variety of 10 mm coloured LEDs
- small button batteries
- momentary switch (or any switch)
- wire
- vinyl tubing
- electrical tape
- electrical wire

Turn it on!

① To operate the LED, we will wire a switch into the circuit. This can be any type of switch, but a momentary switch works best. If your switch has two terminals, you need to solder a 5 cm wire onto one terminal and a 25 cm onto the other.

If your switch has four terminals, look for markings on the underside of your switch to determine which terminals to connect. If you are unsure you can always test out your circuit using a breadboard before you start soldering.

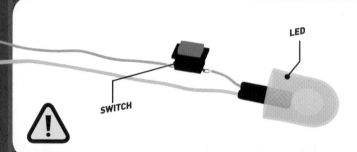

LED

SWITCH

② Next, solder one leg of the LED to the 5 cm wire that goes to the switch. Solder a new 30 cm lead to the other leg of the LED. You almost have a complete circuit – you just need a battery to power the LED.

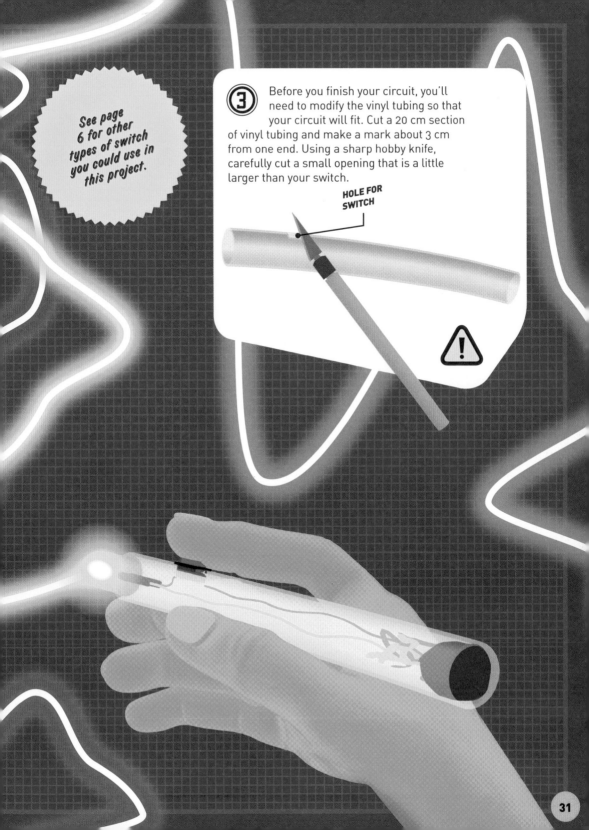

See page 6 for other types of switch you could use in this project.

3 Before you finish your circuit, you'll need to modify the vinyl tubing so that your circuit will fit. Cut a 20 cm section of vinyl tubing and make a mark about 3 cm from one end. Using a sharp hobby knife, carefully cut a small opening that is a little larger than your switch.

HOLE FOR SWITCH

4 Push the LED into the end of the vinyl tubing nearest the switch hole and feed the wires through to the other end, positioning the switch in the hole you cut with the sharp hobby knife.

You should now have a vinyl tube with an LED at one end, a switch in the middle and two wires sticking out of the other end.

Push wires out of opposite end to LED

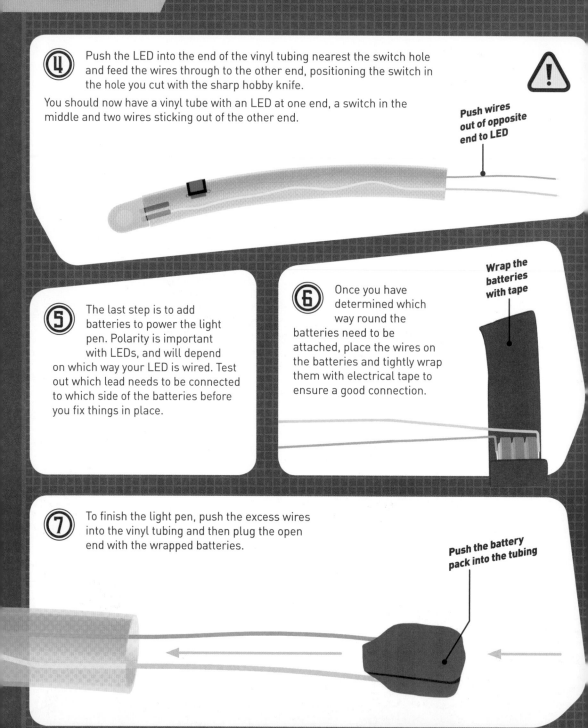

5 The last step is to add batteries to power the light pen. Polarity is important with LEDs, and will depend on which way your LED is wired. Test out which lead needs to be connected to which side of the batteries before you fix things in place.

6 Once you have determined which way round the batteries need to be attached, place the wires on the batteries and tightly wrap them with electrical tape to ensure a good connection.

Wrap the batteries with tape

7 To finish the light pen, push the excess wires into the vinyl tubing and then plug the open end with the wrapped batteries.

Push the battery pack into the tubing

8 The battery plug, LED and switch can all be fixed to the vinyl tube with a small dab of hot glue to ensure they stay in place. Test your light pen with a few presses of the momentary switch, and you're done!

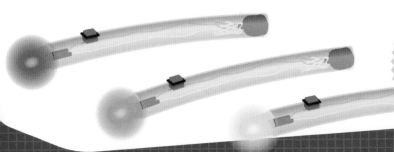

Make a few light pens of different colours and create your own masterpiece!

How to take light pen pictures

You'll need a dark room so the light pens really shine. You'll also need a tripod to keep your camera steady.

Most point-and-shoot cameras have a 'night mode' that allows the camera to capture more light in dark environments. Manual cameras have a setting to allow the shutter to stay open longer. The 'bulb' setting will allow the shutter to stay open indefinitely. What we're looking for is a picture with a long exposure.

Turn off all the lights and take your long exposure picture. With the camera in action, get in front and start drawing your picture with your light pen, pressing the switch to activate the LED and letting go to turn it off. When you've finished, stop the camera exposure and check out your masterpiece. Keep taking long exposure photos until you've got it picture perfect!

Wire maze

A wire maze is a classic electronics project that demonstrates an open or closed circuit perfectly. You may have seen something like this at a fairground or a science centre. The aim of the game is to move the wand from one end of the maze to the other without touching the wire. If the wand touches the wire the circuit is closed and this creates a buzzing sound, which means you lose!

Get buzzy!

You will need

- **battery holder and 2 AA batteries**
- **3 volt buzzer**
- **stiff conducting wire (uncoated is best)**
- **foamcore board**
- **2 machine screws, with washers and nuts**
- **hot glue**
- **soldering iron and solder**
- **electrical tape**
- **electrical wire**
- **pencil**

Buzzers come in all sorts of shapes and sizes, and with different voltages depending on the size and loudness of the buzzer. Pick one that best suits your project.

1 Test your buzzer by wiring it directly to the batteries – it should make a sound when you complete the circuit.

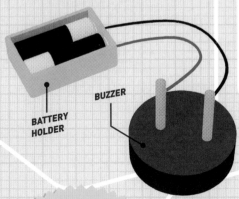

BATTERY HOLDER

BUZZER

2 Cut a section of foamcore board to 30 cm x 15 cm, or a different size if you wish. Poke small openings at either end that are big enough for a machine screw to fit through.

Poke two small holes with a pencil

30 CM

15 CM

In your wire maze, instead of completing a circuit and closing it, you'll want it to stay open until the wand touches the wire and completes the circuit.

3 Completely strip the stiff wire of any vinyl coating it may have – we only want the bare metal wire. Wrap one end of the bare wire around one of the machine screws. Then insert the screw through one of the holes in the foamcore board and fasten with washers and a nut.

TOPSIDE

4 Feed one of the battery wires through the other opening in the foamcore board from the underside and wrap it around the other end of the stiff wire. Then attach the wound wires to a machine screw. Insert the screw through the other hole and secure with a washer and nut as you did in step 3.

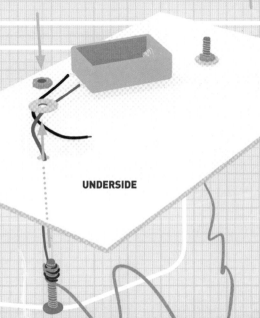

UNDERSIDE

Solder wires
to the buzzer

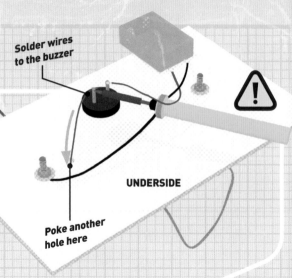

5 Solder one of the buzzer terminals to the other battery wire, then solder a new 30 cm wire to the other buzzer terminal. Create a new opening in the foamcore board. This is where the wand will be placed, so you should make it close to one of the machine screws. Feed the new 30 cm wire through this new hole.

UNDERSIDE

Poke another
hole here

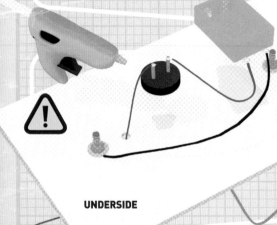

UNDERSIDE

6 You can now secure the battery pack, buzzer and any loose wires to the underside of the foamcore board with hot glue to hold them in place.

7 Adding legs to the underside of the foamcore allows space for the battery and buzzer. Cut twenty 2 cm x 2 cm foamcore squares, then hot glue them into equal stacks of five. These stacks of foamcore will be the legs of the wire maze. Hot glue one stack to each corner on the underside of the foamcore board.

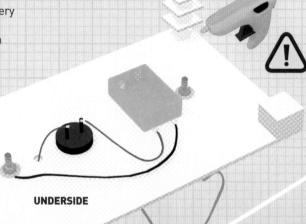

UNDERSIDE

8 To make the wand that goes on the wire maze, strip a 10 cm section of stiff wire and bend it into a loop with a small 5 cm handle. Then solder the handle to the electrical wire that was fed up through the new hole in the foamcore board. Open the loop slightly and place onto the wire maze. Then close the loop. Insert the batteries in the holder that is glued to the underside to activate your wire maze.

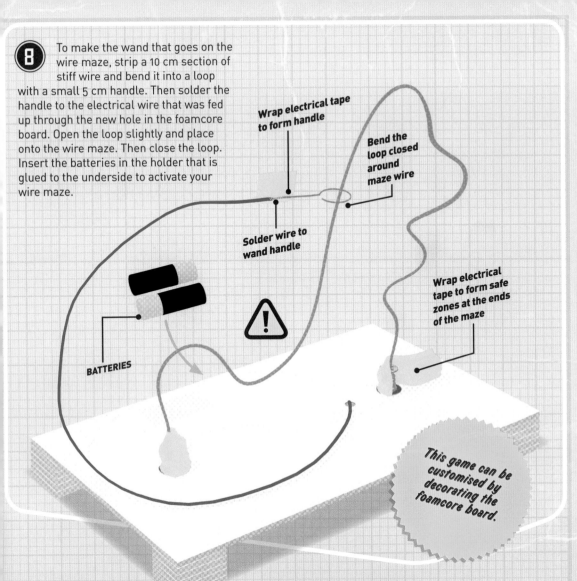

Wrap electrical tape to form handle

Bend the loop closed around maze wire

Solder wire to wand handle

Wrap electrical tape to form safe zones at the ends of the maze

BATTERIES

This game can be customised by decorating the foamcore board.

How it works

When the stiff metal loop comes into contact with the stiff wire maze it will close the circuit and activate the buzzer. The aim of the game is to get the wand loop from one end of the wire maze to the other without making the buzzer sound.

TAKE IT FURTHER

Making things harder

Once you've mastered your original maze, you can add more bends to make things a little trickier. Since the stiff wire is pliable, you can start with easy bends and change it to be a more challenging maze later.

Potato clock

This fun experiment shows that electricity doesn't just come from wall sockets and batteries, but can come from everyday things around us – even the food you eat! In this project we'll use regular potatoes to generate electricity to power a small digital clock.

You will need

- **2 potatoes**
- **small LED clock**
- **2 pieces of heavy copper wire**
- **2 galvanised nails (zinc nails)**
- **electrical tape**
- **electrical wire**
- **6 crocodile clips**

Make sure that the LED clock you use in this project runs on batteries, and not off mains electricity.

10:32

Beat the clock!

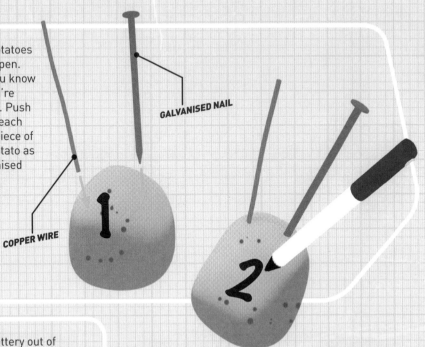

1 Number your potatoes using a marker pen. This will help you know which is which when you're wiring them up in series. Push one galvanised nail into each potato, then insert one piece of copper wire into each potato as far away from the galvanised nail as possible.

GALVANISED NAIL

COPPER WIRE

2 Take the battery out of your LED clock and make a note of the polarity in the battery compartment.

 POSITIVE

 NEGATIVE

3 Fix wires to the crocodile clips. To do this you may have to solder them in place, or use screws that are already on the clips. Attach one crocodile clip to the positive (+) terminal on the LED clock's battery compartment, and another crocodile clip to the negative (-) terminal.

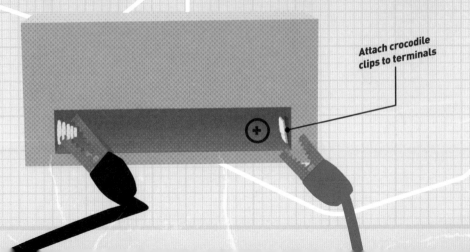

Attach crocodile clips to terminals

4 Now it's time to connect your potatoes. Connect the wire coming from the LED clock's positive terminal to the copper wire on potato number one. Then connect the wire coming from the negative (-) terminal on the LED clock's battery compartment to the galvanised nail on potato number two.

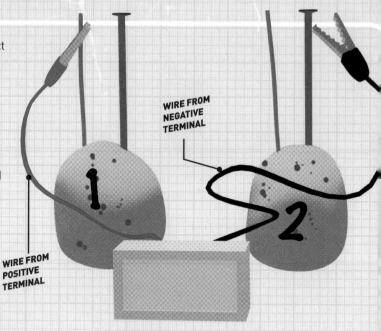

WIRE FROM NEGATIVE TERMINAL

WIRE FROM POSITIVE TERMINAL

5 Lastly, connect two crocodile clips to either end of another wire. Then use this to connect the galvanised nail from potato one to the copper wire on potato two. The circuit is complete!

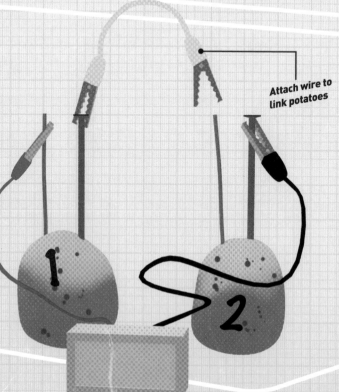

Attach wire to link potatoes

6 As soon as the last connection is made and the circuit is completed, the LED clock should turn on. If your clock doesn't power up, check your connections to ensure good contact. Also, make sure your galvanised nails and copper wires aren't touching inside the potatoes.

You can use other foods to power your clock, including apples, lemons, oranges and tomatoes. Experiment with them all and find out which works best.

How it works

By using a potato to power the clock, we're using what's called an electrochemical battery, or cell. An electrochemical cell is when chemical energy is converted to electrical energy by an electron transfer. In the case of your potato clock, that's when the zinc nail reacts with the copper wire. If the zinc and copper touch each other, they would start the reaction but only generate heat. By adding the potato, we keep the zinc and copper apart and force the transfer of electrons between the two metals through the potato and into the clock to power it.

TAKE IT FURTHER

While this power method is great, it may not last long. But you can boost the power by adding more potatoes and wiring them up as shown – it's just like adding more batteries!

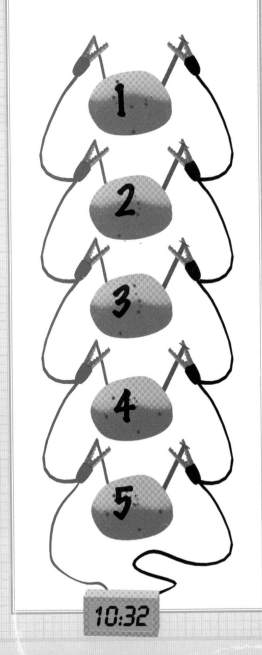

10:32

41

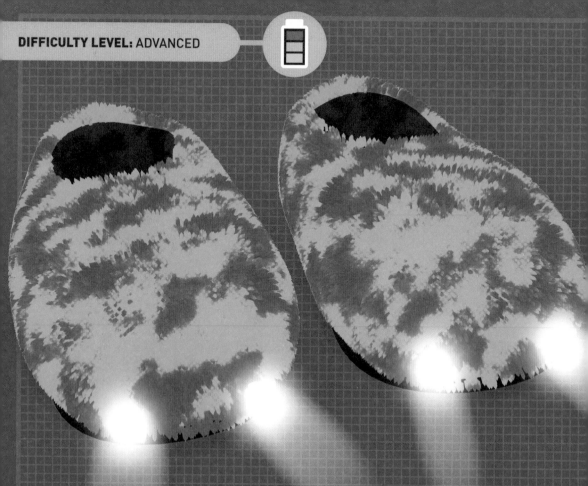

LED slippers

At night, you can keep your feet warm by wearing slippers, but what if you could make your slippers light up and show you the way in the dark? With this project, we'll do just that by adding LEDs to your slippers. They'll shine light in the darkness so you can find your way to the bathroom, or into the kitchen for a late-night snack!

You will need

- slippers
- 4 bright white LEDs
- 2 button cell battery holders
- 2 button cell batteries
- 2 push-button switches
- electrical wire
- soldering iron and solder
- wire coat hanger

Shine a light!

 ① Start by soldering two red 30 cm wires to the positive (+) terminal of the battery holder, then one black 15 cm wire to the negative (-) battery terminal.

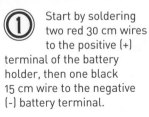

Solder wires to battery holder

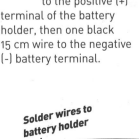

② Solder a push-button switch to the 15 cm wire, then solder another two black 15 cm wires to the other side of the switch. This is most of the circuit complete, we're just missing the LEDs, which we'll add once the wiring is inserted into the slipper.

 ③ Lounge slippers usually have lots of padding around them, so you can put your wires and components in lots of different places. Try putting the battery holder near the side of the heel to keep it out of the way, with the switch on the side of the slipper for easy access. You can choose to place your circuit wherever you like to suit your slippers.

④ Make a small cut in the stitching of the slippers near the back, and a slit about 5 cm long where you want the LEDs in the front of the slippers. Open out the wire coat hanger and push it into the front slit and out through the back of the slippers. The coat hanger will help to guide the wires into the slipper. Wrap the wires from the switch and the battery holder around the coat hanger at the back of the slipper and gently pull them through the slipper until the wires are poking out the front. Then move the switch into place to the side of the slipper.

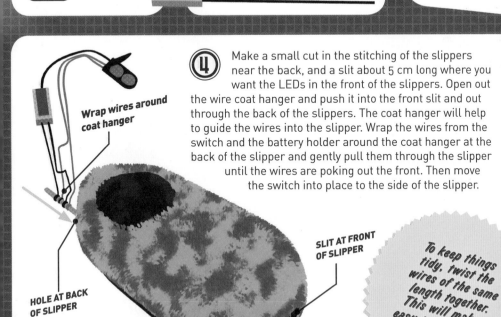

Wrap wires around coat hanger

HOLE AT BACK OF SLIPPER

SLIT AT FRONT OF SLIPPER

To keep things tidy, twist the wires of the same length together. This will make it easy to insert them into the slipper.

5 The battery holder and any excess wires can be pushed into the opening last. It may take a little time and effort to manoeuvre the wires into place. If you get stuck you can make additional openings in the slipper seams to help put the wires in place – just sew them closed afterwards. Make sure you don't sew the battery compartment closed just yet.

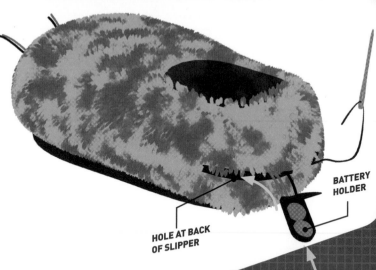

BATTERY HOLDER

HOLE AT BACK OF SLIPPER

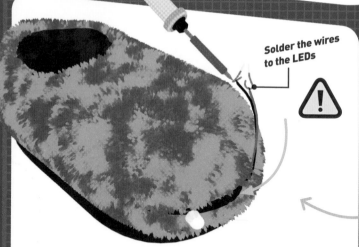

Solder the wires to the LEDs

6 Now connect the LEDs to the wires at the front of the slippers. There are four wires poking out the front, two red and two black. Solder the long leg of one LED to one of the red wires, then the short leg of that LED to one black wire. This is one of the LED circuits completed. Solder the other LED to the remaining red and black wires in the same way. The LEDs can now be inserted at either end of the slit at the front of the slipper.

Troubleshooter

If your slipper is really large and has lots of padding inside the toe, you may need to add a small base to the LEDs to make them point in the right direction when inserted into the slipper. You can easily do this by cutting a small disc from some cardboard or cardstock, making a small opening in the centre to put the LED inside, and then hot-glueing it into place. The LED and card disc can then be inserted into the slipper. Sew the LED openings shut, but keep enough of an opening to allow the LED to shine through.

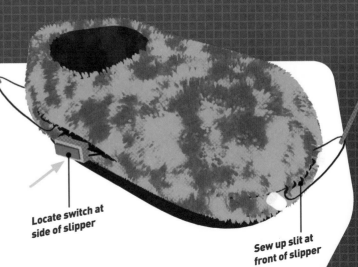

7 Sew up the slit at the front of the slipper to hold the LEDs in place. Locate where the switch is inside the slipper and make a small opening where you want the button to be located. Pull the wires around until you bring the switch out of the slipper and sew the opening closed with the switch outside.

Locate switch at side of slipper

Sew up slit at front of slipper

8 You can now insert the batteries into the battery holder and test your circuit by clicking the switch. Sew the battery holder in place and repeat the same steps for the other slipper and get ready for night vision!

Remember to position the switch on the opposite side for the other slipper!

TAKE IT FURTHER

On and off

If you want to test your electronic skills, you can combine this project with the DIY switch from pages 18–19, which replaces the push button switch with a momentary switch. If you place this under your heel, then the LEDs will only activate when you're standing on that foot, so they will turn on and off each time you take a step.

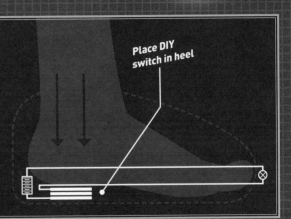

Place DIY switch in heel

Drawing robot

One of the best things about electronics is making robots. You can make robots in any shape you like, to perform all kinds of fun things. Make a few and have an army of robots, ready to do your bidding!

You will need

- computer fan (9 volts and 120 mm)
- 4 or more felt tip markers
- 9 volt battery with snap connector
- elastic bands
- pliers
- soldering iron and solder
- electrical wire

You can customise this robot by adding more markers or by using markers with different thicknesses.

Get squiggling!

1 Start by finding an old computer fan – look for a large 120 mm fan that runs on 9 volts. You can tell what the fan voltage is as it's printed on the fan casing. Your computer fan will have wires coming from the case, and sometimes these wires have a plastic connector tip. You can clip the connector off and then strip the ends of the wires in preparation for connecting the battery.

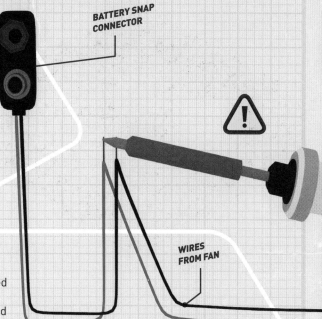

BATTERY SNAP CONNECTOR

WIRES FROM FAN

2 A 9 volt battery snap connector is a cap that snaps onto the top of a battery with two wires. Leave the battery disconnected for now, but you can connect the wires to the fan wires. The battery wires will be red and black, and the wires from your fan will be colour coded in the same way. Match the wire colours and twist them together – black to black and red to red. Then solder your wires to make a secure connection. You can test your connections by plugging your battery into the snap connectors to see if the fan spins.

3 Using pliers, carefully cut off two or three of the fan blades. This will make the fan spin erratically and produce some fun designs. Start by cutting a few blades off and come back to cut more later if you want your robot to make even crazier designs. Remember, while you can cut off more blades, you can't put them back on. So, start small.

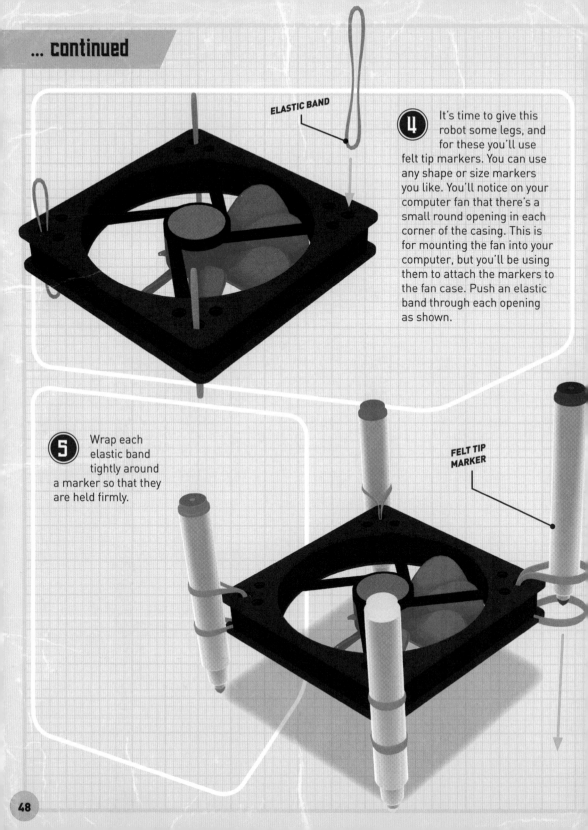

ELASTIC BAND

4 It's time to give this robot some legs, and for these you'll use felt tip markers. You can use any shape or size markers you like. You'll notice on your computer fan that there's a small round opening in each corner of the casing. This is for mounting the fan into your computer, but you'll be using them to attach the markers to the fan case. Push an elastic band through each opening as shown.

5 Wrap each elastic band tightly around a marker so that they are held firmly.

FELT TIP MARKER

6 Use some hot glue to stick the 9 volt battery to the centre of the fan casing (not the spinning side of the fan!).

7 Once the glue has cooled and hardened, connect the battery. Your drawing robot should start jittering and vibrating around, place it on a large sheet of paper and watch it skitter around and leave squiggly artwork.

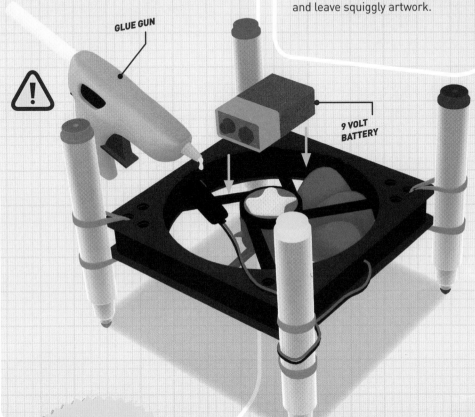

GLUE GUN

9 VOLT BATTERY

Ask an adult for permission before using hot glue or solder and make sure they are with you to help. Don't forget to follow all the soldering instructions on pages 12–13.

TAKE IT FURTHER

Mixing it up

You can customise this robot by leaving a marker cap or two on the markers. You could also try placing one of the legs onto an eraser. This will hold that leg in place, making the scribbling robot spin around.

Wall robot

Take your robots to the next level and make them climb vertical surfaces. By using a small fridge magnet, you can make your robot crawl along any metal or magnetic surface, such as fridges, black or whiteboards, or a metal door.

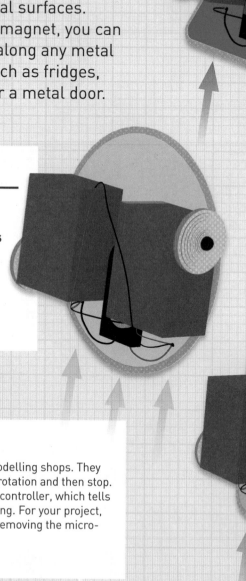

You will need

- **2 small servo motors**
- **fridge magnet**
- **2 button cell 1.5 volt batteries**
- **button cell battery holder**
- **2 thick elastic bands**
- **heat-shrink tubing**
- **electrical wire**

Servo motors

Servo motors can be bought from modelling shops. They are motors that perform a specified rotation and then stop. They are made to work with a micro-controller, which tells them when to operate and for how long. For your project, you'll be keeping things simple and removing the micro-controller interface from the servos.

Climbing the walls

1 Start by prying or unscrewing the back of the servo casing open. The first thing you should see is the control board.

UNDERSIDE

CONTROL BOARD

2 Most control boards will have a three-wire ribbon cable attached – two wires are to provide power and the third is a control signal wire.

De-solder wires from the motor

THREE-WIRE RIBBON CABLE

SERVO MOTOR

3 Leave the three-wire ribbon cable and de-solder the two wires connected to the control board (not the three-wire ribbon). This should detach any connection between the control board and the servo, allowing the control board and three-wire ribbon to be removed as one.

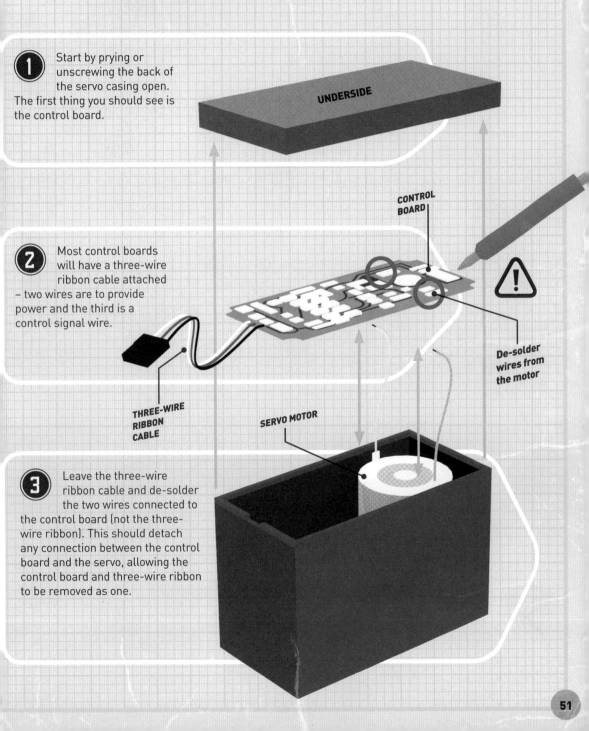

4 Solder new different-coloured wires directly to the motor wires. Protect the wires from shorting out by sealing the joins in heat-shrink tubing. Tuck the soldered connection into the servo housing and snap the underside of the servo box back on. Repeat steps 1 to 4 to create a second motor.

UNDERSIDE

HEAT-SHRINK TUBING

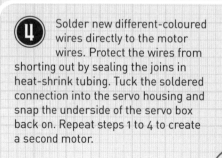

5 The hardest part is done! Use hot glue to attach the servo motors to the weak fridge magnet. Stick the servos on straight so that your robot's motor shafts are aligned and it climbs straight.

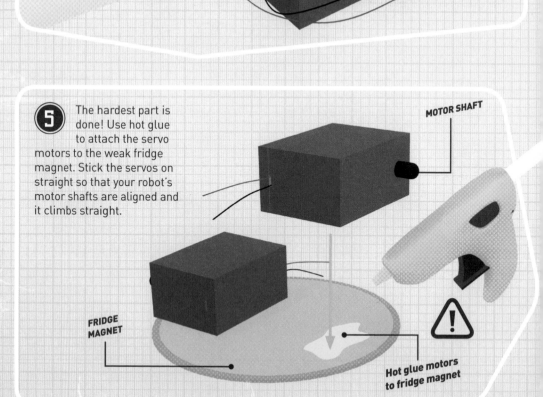

MOTOR SHAFT

FRIDGE MAGNET

Hot glue motors to fridge magnet

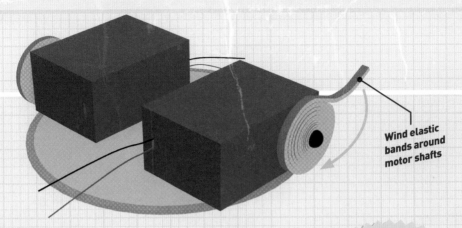

Wind elastic bands around motor shafts

6 Cut the elastic bands and lay them flat. Use a small dab of hot glue on the motor shaft and wind the elastic band onto the shaft creating a wheel. Use another small dab of hot glue to secure the end of the elastic band to stop it unwinding. Repeat this on the other motor shaft.

If we were to wire the servos up now, they would be spinning in opposite directions, since they are on opposing sides of the fridge magnet chassis!

7 Next, we will reverse the polarity of one of the motors, making it spin in the opposite direction so that your robot will travel in a straight path. If you were using the standard red and black wires soldered to the servo motors in step 4, you should match one black and one red from each and wind them together. Hot glue the battery holder to the magnet. Solder the black and red paired wires to the battery holder, and you're done!

Troubleshooter

Is your magnet too strong to allow the robot to move along the metal surface? No problem! By sticking a few small squares of paper on top of the magnet you'll create a gap between the magnet and the metal surface and weaken the magnetic attraction. This should allow your robot to stick to a vertical metal surface but still climb it.

Hot glue the battery holder in place

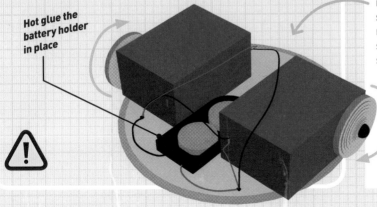

This bookmark can be customised by decorating it. You should do this before you start so that it doesn't affect the electrical components.

LED bookmark

Reading is always great, but sometimes you don't have the light you need to continue reading. This LED bookmark will solve that problem. It will save your place in your reading material and light the words so you can continue reading in the dark.

You will need

- **button cell battery holder**
- **button cell battery**
- **2 bright white LEDs**
- **SPST switch**
- **cereal box**
- **scissors**
- **wire cutters**
- **hot glue**
- **marker pen**
- **pin or sewing needle**
- **electrical wire**

Shine a light!

1 You can make your bookmark any size you like, but it should be at least 4 cm x 10 cm so that it's big enough to hold the electronics. Cut two rectangles from your cereal box the size you want for your bookmark. Then glue the two sides together with the images facing inwards, leaving you with the plain surfaces on the outside.

2 Mark the long LED legs with a marker pen so you know which end is positive (+). Then trim the long positive LED leg so that the two legs are the same length.

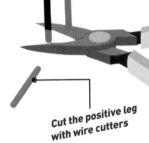

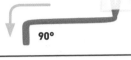

Cut the positive leg with wire cutters

When bending the legs of your LEDs, make sure that the positive and negative legs will line up with each other when you join them together.

LED 1

90°

90°

LED 2

90°

90°

3 Bend the LED legs 90 degrees and flat against the underside of the LED. Then bend the last 5 mm of the legs at right angles away from the LED.

Repeat with the second LED, but make each bend in the opposite direction to the first LED, so they are mirrored, as shown.

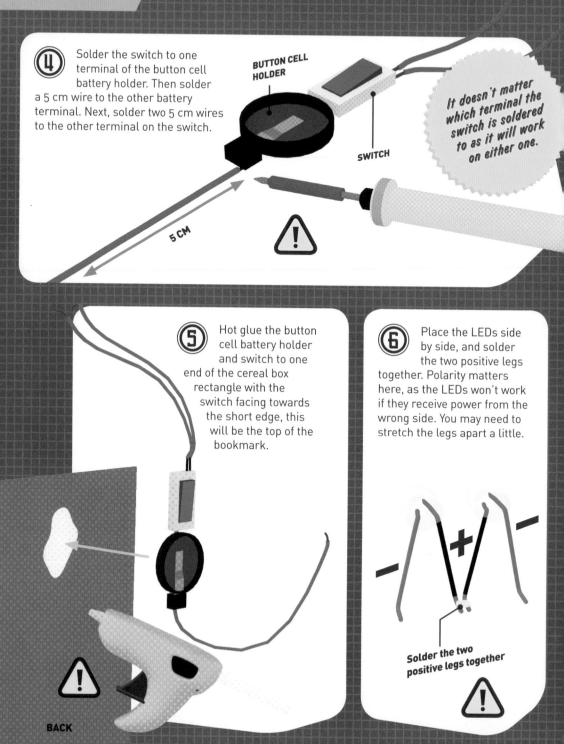

④ Solder the switch to one terminal of the button cell battery holder. Then solder a 5 cm wire to the other battery terminal. Next, solder two 5 cm wires to the other terminal on the switch.

BUTTON CELL HOLDER

SWITCH

It doesn't matter which terminal the switch is soldered to as it will work on either one.

5 CM

⑤ Hot glue the button cell battery holder and switch to one end of the cereal box rectangle with the switch facing towards the short edge, this will be the top of the bookmark.

BACK

⑥ Place the LEDs side by side, and solder the two positive legs together. Polarity matters here, as the LEDs won't work if they receive power from the wrong side. You may need to stretch the legs apart a little.

Solder the two positive legs together

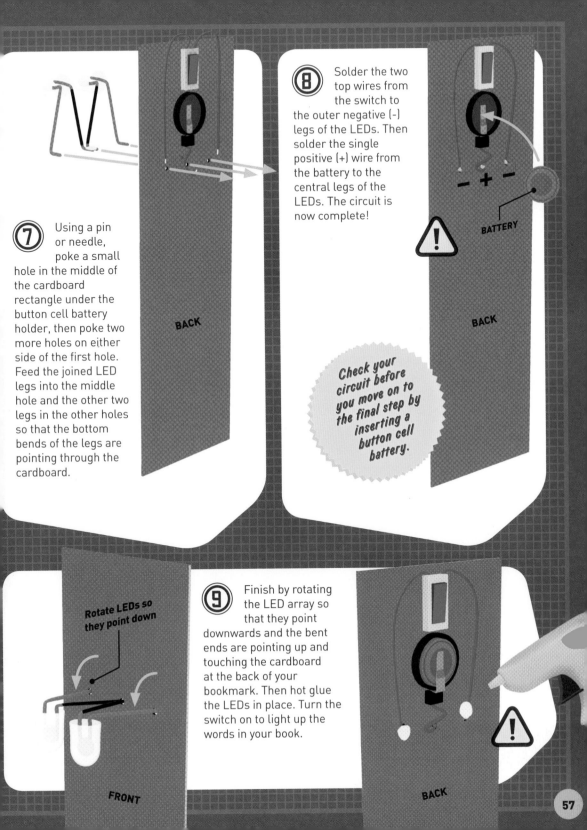

8 Solder the two top wires from the switch to the outer negative (-) legs of the LEDs. Then solder the single positive (+) wire from the battery to the central legs of the LEDs. The circuit is now complete!

BATTERY

BACK

7 Using a pin or needle, poke a small hole in the middle of the cardboard rectangle under the button cell battery holder, then poke two more holes on either side of the first hole. Feed the joined LED legs into the middle hole and the other two legs in the other holes so that the bottom bends of the legs are pointing through the cardboard.

BACK

Check your circuit before you move on to the final step by inserting a button cell battery.

Rotate LEDs so they point down

9 Finish by rotating the LED array so that they point downwards and the bent ends are pointing up and touching the cardboard at the back of your bookmark. Then hot glue the LEDs in place. Turn the switch on to light up the words in your book.

FRONT

BACK

Pocket torch

Torches are incredibly useful tools, but sometimes we don't know we need them until the lights are already out. Making a very small pocket torch allows you to keep a light source with you at all times, ready for the next time you are plunged into darkness.

A light in the dark

You will need

- **2 bright white LEDs**
- **2 LED holders**
- **plastic bottle cap**
- **momentary switch**
- **button cell battery**
- **soldering iron and solder**
- **electrical tape**
- **soldering tip cleaner**
- **thin piece of foam or plastic**
- **hot glue**
- **electrical wire**

Ask an adult to supervise you during this stage and make sure that the room you are in has plenty of ventilation.

① Heat up your soldering iron and carefully push the hot tip through the side of the plastic bottle cap to make a round opening. Then make another round hole next to the first as close as possible, but without the two openings overlapping and becoming one.

② With the iron still hot, poke an opening in the centre of the bottle cap top. This will be the opening for the momentary switch, so make sure it is large enough to have the switch button sticking out through the top of the cap. Clean the tip of your soldering iron once you have done this.

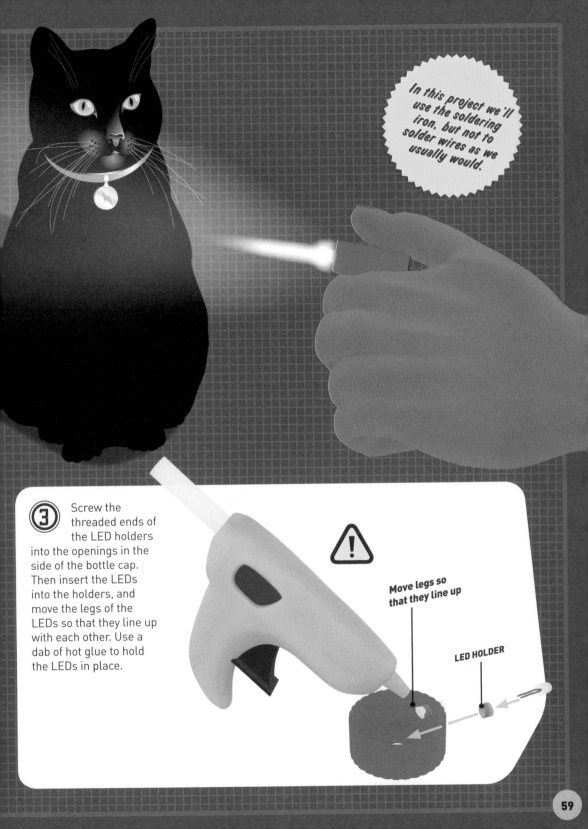

In this project we'll use the soldering iron, but not to solder wires as we usually would.

3 Screw the threaded ends of the LED holders into the openings in the side of the bottle cap. Then insert the LEDs into the holders, and move the legs of the LEDs so that they line up with each other. Use a dab of hot glue to hold the LEDs in place.

Move legs so that they line up

LED HOLDER

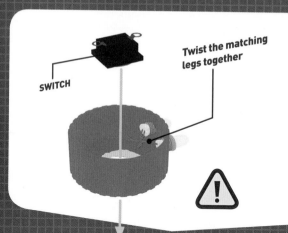

SWITCH

Twist the matching legs together

 Twist the long legs of the LEDs together, then twist the short legs together. Move both pairs of legs out of the way to install the switch. Place the momentary switch into the top opening of the soda cap and use hot glue to fix it in place.

 Make sure there are no bits of melted plastic on the soldering iron. Then solder one set of LED legs to one terminal of the momentary switch. Next, solder a small section of wire to the other terminal of the momentary switch. This will eventually connect to the battery. Cut a small piece of electrical tape and cover the connections of the switch and the soldered LEDs.

ELECTRICAL TAPE

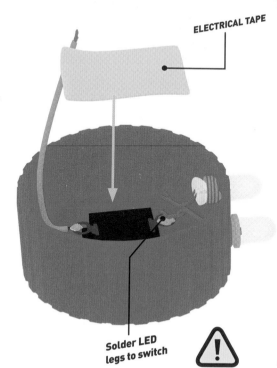

It doesn't matter which set of LED legs you solder to the momentary switch, since you can change the polarity to match the battery to match the LEDs.

Solder LED legs to switch

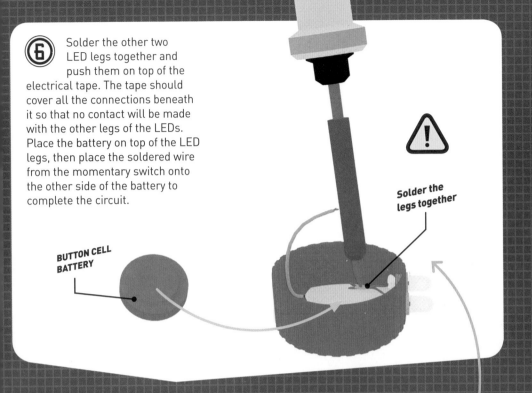

6 Solder the other two LED legs together and push them on top of the electrical tape. The tape should cover all the connections beneath it so that no contact will be made with the other legs of the LEDs. Place the battery on top of the LED legs, then place the soldered wire from the momentary switch onto the other side of the battery to complete the circuit.

BUTTON CELL BATTERY

Solder the legs together

7 Holding the wire against the battery, check that you've got the connections the right way round by pressing the momentary switch. If your circuit is good, you can use electrical tape to hold the wire against the battery. Then seal the bottle cap with another piece of thin plastic or foam to hide all the components and hold everything in place. Push the button to activate your torch and light up the dark!

Troubleshooter

If your LED doesn't light up immediately, but your battery is the correct way round then maybe you've got a short circuit. Check that the electrical tape is completely covering the LED and switch connection beneath the battery.

Glossary

Alternating Current (AC) flow of electricity that reverses direction many times a second

amp standard unit of measurement for the strength of an electrical current

breadboard construction base used for testing out electrical circuits (originally formed out of a piece of wood)

button cell battery small battery shaped like a button that is used to power small portable electronic devices

conductive thread thread that can carry electrical current in the same way wire can

control board panel containing switches, dials and other equipment for regulating electrical devices

current movement of electricity in a particular direction

Direct Current (DC) flow of electricity that moves in one direction only

electrical circuit path of electrical current that begins with a battery, then goes through various components and ends up back at the battery through an unbroken connection

electrochemical cell or battery enables chemical energy to convert to electrical energy by an electron transfer

ferromagnetic material that has the same type of magnetism as iron

LED abbreviation for light-emitting diode. This is a small component that produces light on electrical equipment or in a circuit.

momentary switch type of switch that completes an electrical circuit, but only for a moment. It works only when pressed.

parallel circuit components wired into a parallel circuit share polarity on a common side and receive the same voltage

polarity direction of electrical current in a circuit. Currents flow from the positive pole to the negative pole.

rare-earth magnet strong permanent magnet made from the rare-earth alloys neodymium, iron and boron

resistance degree to which an electrical current is restricted in its flow, or movement

series circuit components in a series circuit are wired like a daisy-chain, which means that each component receives the same amount of electrical current

servo motor type of motor that performs a specified rotation and then stops

soldering use of heat and metal with a low melting point to join things, such as wires, together

SPDT switch Single Pole Double Throw switch controls two circuits. Single pole means there is only one way to pull the switch: on and off.

SPST switch Single Pole Single Throw switch controls one circuit

terminal point at which connection can be made to an electrical component. For example, a battery has two terminals: positive and negative.

tinning application of solder prior to soldering

voltage force of an electrical current measured in volts. A volt is the measure of electric pressure, often supplied by a battery.

RESOURCES

www.instructables.com/id/ Electronic-Projects-For-Beginners
Open source projects made by other gadget inventors. A great place for inspiration and taking projects to the next level.

www.circuitstoday.com/simple- electronics-projects-and-circuits
More advanced projects that use the same skills learned in this book!

www.learn.sparkfun.com/tutorials
A great resource for advanced projects, and a shop to buy components.

littlebits.cc
Pre-made electronic building blocks that allow easy prototyping. A great tool to invest in if you're looking to explore new components and how they work together.

www.makercamp.com/projects
Fun projects to make ranging from easy to challenging, all with the young inventor in mind.

Index